SCHOLASTIC

Writing Lessons to Meet the Common Core

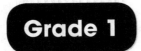
Grade 1

Linda Ward Beech

NEW YORK ● TORONTO ● LONDON ● AUCKLAND ● SYDNEY
MEXICO CITY ● NEW DELHI ● HONG KONG ● BUENOS AIRES

Teaching Resources

Cover design by Scott Davis
Interior design by Kathy Massaro
Illustrations by Maxie Chambliss, Rusty Fletcher, Anne Kennedy, and Bari Weissman

ISBN: 978-0-545-49597-4

3   4   5   6   7   8   9   10   40   20   19   18   17   16   15   14

Contents

About This Book

To build a foundation for college and career readiness, students need to learn to use writing as a way of offering and supporting opinions, demonstrating understanding of the subjects they are studying, and conveying real and imagined experiences and events. They learn to appreciate that a key purpose of writing is to communicate clearly to an external, sometimes unfamiliar audience, and they begin to adapt the form and content of their writing to accomplish a particular task and purpose.

—COMMON CORE STATE STANDARDS FOR ENGLISH LANGUAGE ARTS, JUNE 2010

Support for First Graders

The first two lessons in each section of grade 1 focus on an important skill—fact and opinion for opinion writing, main idea for informative writing, and sequence for narrative writing. These introductory lessons provide the scaffolding students need to be successful in each of these writing forms.

This book includes step-by-step instructions for teaching the three forms of writing—Opinion, Informative/Explanatory, and Narrative—covered in the Common Core State Standards (CCSS). The CCSS are a result of a state-led effort to establish a single set of clear educational standards aimed at providing students nationwide with a high-quality education. The standards outline the knowledge and skills that students should achieve during their years in school.

The writing standards are a subset of the Common Core English Language Arts Standards. They provide "a focus for instruction" to help students gain a mastery of a range of skills and applications necessary for writing clear prose. This book is divided into three main sections; each section includes six lessons devoted to one of the writing forms covered in the CCSS for grade 1. You'll find more about each of these types of writing on pages 6–7.

- **Lessons 1–6** (pages 8–25) focus on the skills and standards for writing opinion pieces.
- **Lessons 7–12** (pages 26–43) emphasize skills and standards particular to informative/explanatory writing.
- **Lessons 13–18** (pages 44–61) address the skills and standards for narrative writing.

Although the CCSS do not specify how to teach any form of writing, the lessons in this book follow the gradual release of responsibility model of instruction: I Do It, We Do It, You Do It (Pearson & Gallagher, 1983). This model provides educators with a framework for releasing responsibility to students in a gradual manner. It recognizes that we learn best when a concept is demonstrated to us; when we have sufficient time to practice it with support; and when we are then given the opportunity to try it on our own. Each phase is equally important, but the chief goal is to teach for independence—the You Do It phase—so that students really learn to take over the skill and apply it in new situations.

Pearson, P. D., & Gallagher, M. C. (1983). "The Instruction of Reading Comprehension." *Contemporary Educational Psychology*, 8 (3).

A Look at the Lessons

The lessons in each section progress in difficulty and increase in the number of objectives and standards covered. This format enables you to use beginning or later lessons in a section depending on your students' abilities. Each lesson includes a list of the objectives and standards included. A general reproducible offering students an assessment checklist of standards for each writing form appears at the end of the book. (See pages 62–64.)

Here's a look at the features in each lesson.

Lesson Page 1

The first page is the teaching page of each lesson. It provides a step-by-step plan for using the student reproducible on the second lesson page and the On Your Own activity on the third lesson page. The teaching page closely follows the organization of the student reproducibles. This page also models sample text that students might generate when completing page 2 of the lesson. Finally, the teaching page includes an opportunity for students to review their classmates' work using the reproducible assessment checklist or a list customized to the lesson's writing form. Each checklist also reminds students to check for correct punctuation and spelling.

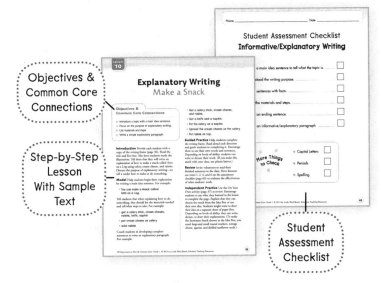

Objectives & Common Core Connections

Step-by-Step Lesson With Sample Text

Student Assessment Checklist

Lesson Page 2

The second page is a student reproducible, which is the core of the lesson. Students complete this writing frame as you guide them. In some lessons, students use the completed page as the basis for a paragraph they write on a separate sheet of paper.

> Although you provide a model for completing this reproducible, you'll want to encourage students to use their own ideas, words, and sentences as much as possible.

Introduction

Instructions

Writing Task

Lesson Page 3

The third page is a writing frame for independent work. It follows a format similar to the one students used for the first reproducible. Students choose their topic from those suggested or use their own idea for the topic. In some lessons, students use the completed page as the basis for a paragraph they write on a separate sheet of paper.

Introduction

Topic Suggestions

Writing Task

Three Forms of Writing

The CCSS focus on three forms of writing—opinion, informative/explanatory, and narrative.

Opinion Writing (Standard W.1.1)

The purpose of writing opinion pieces is to convince others to think or act in a certain way, to encourage readers or listeners to share the writer's point of view, beliefs, or position. Opinion pieces are also known as persuasive writing.

Hot food is the best way to stay warm.

In developing an opinion piece, students must learn to introduce the topic, present a point of view, and supply valid reasons, facts, and expert opinions to support it. Phrases such as *I think, I believe, you should/should not* all signal persuasive writing.

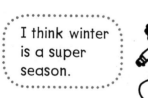

I think winter is a super season.

When teaching these lessons, display different examples of opinion pieces. You might include:

- book, movie, and TV reviews
- print advertisements
- letters in children's publications

As students learn to produce different forms of writing, they are also enhancing their ability to recognize these forms in their reading.

Informative/Explanatory Writing (Standard W.1.2)

The purpose of informative/explanatory writing is to inform the reader by giving facts, explanations, and other information. Informative/explanatory writing is also called expository writing.

When writing an informative/explanatory text, students must introduce the topic and give facts, details, descriptions, and other information about the topic. The information should also be organized in a logical way. Many kinds of informative/explanatory writing require research. Sometimes illustrations are included with informative/explanatory texts.

An apple grows on a tree.

Here is how to draw a turkey.

Display different examples of informative/explanatory writing. You might include:

- reports
- news articles
- how-to articles
- biographies
- directions
- textbooks
- magazines
- recipes

Writing Lessons to Meet the Common Core: Grade 1 © 2013 by Linda Ward Beech, Scholastic Teaching Resources

Narrative Writing (Standard W.1.3)

The purpose of narrative writing is to entertain. A narrative gives an account or a story. Usually, a narrative tells about something that happens over a period of time. Narratives can be true or imaginary.

YaYa ate some bamboo for a snack.

When working on a narrative, students must develop a real or imagined experience or event. They must also establish a situation or plot, create characters, and recount events in a chronological sequence. Narratives usually include descriptive details. Many include dialogue.

Pepe got a baby dinosaur for his birthday.

When introducing narrative writing, display different examples. You might include:

- picture books
- storybooks
- mysteries
- fables
- fairy tales
- folktales
- science fiction
- friendly letters

Additional Writing Standards

Although this book focuses on the forms of writing called for in the CCSS, you can also incorporate the standards that relate to the production and distribution of writing and research to build and present knowledge. These standards include:

- W.1.5 Focus on a topic, respond to questions and suggestions from peers, and add details to strengthen writing as needed.

- W.1.6 Use a variety of digital tools to produce and publish writing.

- W.1.7 Participate in shared research and writing projects to produce a sequence of instructions.

- W.1.8 Recall information from experiences and gather information from provided sources.

Language Standards

In addition, you can incorporate the CCSS Language Standards that focus on the conventions of standard English grammar and usage (L.1.1) and the conventions of standard English capitalization, punctuation, and spelling (L.1.2).

Writing Lessons to Meet the Common Core: Grade 1 © 2013 by Linda Ward Beech, Scholastic Teaching Resources

Opinion Writing (Fact & Opinion)
Mittens

Objectives & Common Core Connections

* Differentiate between fact and opinion.
* Develop facts and opinions about a topic.

Introduction Provide each student with a copy of the fact and opinion writing frame (page 9). Read the title and first lines. Tell students that when you want others to agree with you, you have to persuade them to think the way you do. You have to convince them to share your opinion. Explain that an opinion is a point of view or what someone thinks.

Model Tell students that an opinion about mittens might be stated in a sentence. Review that a sentence is a group of words that tells what someone or something thinks or does. For example:

* I think mittens are great.

Explain that opinions often begin with words such as *I think*. Opinions may also include words such as *best*. For example:

* I think mittens are warmer than gloves.
* Red mittens are the best kind.

Point out that writers need to offer more than an opinion to get others to agree with them; they need to give reasons to support an opinion. To help students understand what kinds of reasons to use, you might say: *Often the reasons a writer gives are facts about the subject.* Explain that a fact is a statement that can be proved. Give examples of statements of fact such as:

* Mittens come in pairs.
* Mittens are for your hands.

Guided Practice Work with students to help them complete the fact and opinion writing frame. Discuss why each item in Part A is an opinion or a fact. For example, Statement 1 is an opinion because it tells what someone thinks. Another person might think that canvas or cloth mittens are the best. Statement 2 is a fact that can be proved. The picture shows that mittens have thumbs.

For Part B, invite students to color the mittens any way they want. This will give them more information to work with as they develop a statement of opinion and a statement of fact. Review that a sentence begins with a capital letter and usually ends with a period. Depending on levels of ability, students can dictate or write their sentences. For example:

Opinion: I think all students need striped mittens.

Fact: Mittens keep hands warm.

Review Check students' work to see that they completed Part A correctly—facts: 2, 3, 5; opinions: 1, 4. Invite volunteers to read their sentences from Part B to the class. Have listeners use these criteria to assess other students' work:

✔ Developed an opinion about the topic
✔ Included a fact about the topic

Independent Practice Use the On Your Own activity (page 10) as review. Encourage students to use what they learned in the lesson to complete the page. They can refer to the pictures of hats to develop statements of opinion and fact. Check students' work to see that they completed Part A correctly—facts: 1, 3; opinions: 2, 4, 5. Depending on levels of ability, students can dictate or write their sentences for Part B.

Mittens

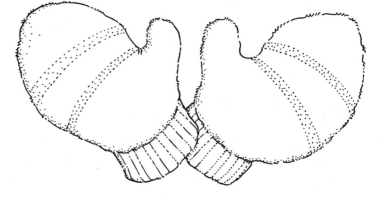

★ What do you know about mittens?
What do you think about them?

A. Write **fact** or **opinion** next to each sentence.

1. _____ Wool mittens are the best kind.

2. _____ Mittens have thumbs.

3. _____ Mittens do not have fingers.

4. _____ I think it is too easy to lose mittens.

5. _____ Mittens are for cold days.

B. Write an opinion and a fact about mittens.

Opinion _____

_____

_____

Fact _____

_____

_____

On Your Own

What do you know about hats?
What do you think about them?

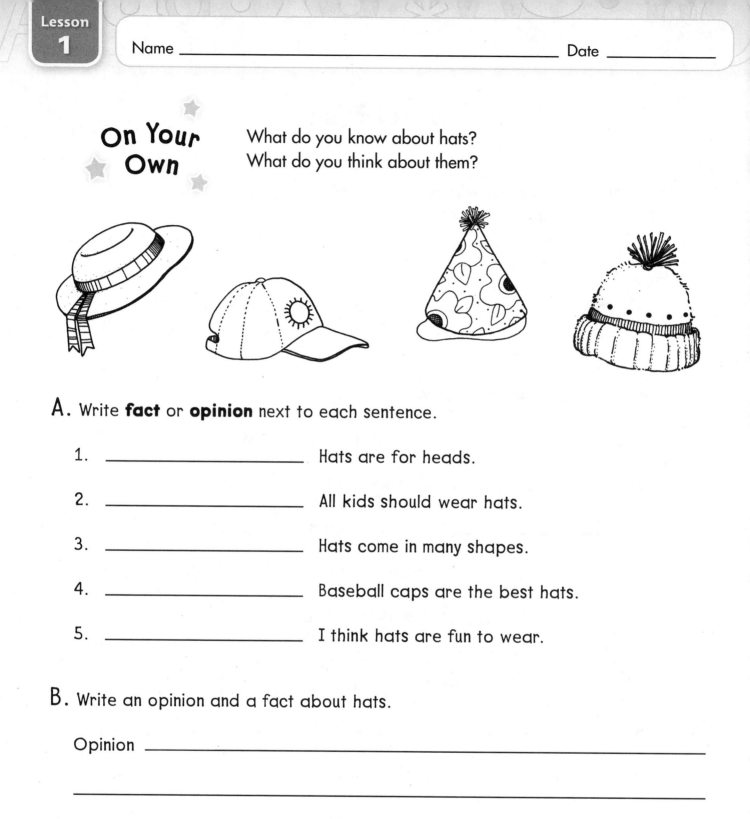

A. Write **fact** or **opinion** next to each sentence.

1. _____ Hats are for heads.

2. _____ All kids should wear hats.

3. _____ Hats come in many shapes.

4. _____ Baseball caps are the best hats.

5. _____ I think hats are fun to wear.

B. Write an opinion and a fact about hats.

Opinion _____

_____

_____

Fact _____

_____

_____

Opinion Writing (Fact & Opinion)
Colors

Objectives & Common Core Connections

❋ Differentiate between fact and opinion.

❋ Develop facts and opinions about a topic.

Introduction Provide each student with a copy of the fact and opinion writing frame (page 12). Read the title and first lines. Tell students that when you want others to agree with you, you have to persuade them to think the way you do. You have to convince them to share your opinion. Explain that an opinion is a point of view or what someone thinks.

Model Tell students that an opinion about the color blue might be stated in a sentence. Review that a sentence is a group of words that tells what someone or something thinks or does. For example:

- I think blue eyes are pretty.

Explain that opinions often begin with words such as *I think*. Opinions may also include words such as *should*, *best*, or *most*. For example:

- Blue is the best color for jeans.
- Red is the most cheerful color.

Point out that writers need to offer more than an opinion to get others to agree with them; they need to give reasons to support an opinion. To help students recognize supportive reasons, you might say: *Often the reasons a writer gives are facts about the subject.* Explain that a fact is a statement that can be proved. Give examples of statements of fact such as:

- A stop sign is red.
- Some birds are blue.

Guided Practice Work with students to help them complete the fact and opinion writing frame. Begin by having them color the crayons red and blue. Discuss why each item in Part A is an opinion or a fact. For example, Statement 1 is an opinion because it tells what someone thinks. Statement 2 is a fact that can be proved.

For Part B, help students develop a statement of opinion and a statement of fact. Review that a sentence begins with a capital letter and usually ends with a period. Depending on levels of ability, students can dictate or write their sentences. For example:

Opinion: I think red is a great color.

Fact: Ink can be blue.

Review Check students' work to see that they completed Part A correctly—facts: 2, 3; opinions: 1, 4, 5. Invite volunteers to read their sentences from Part B to the class. Have listeners use these criteria to assess other students' work:

✔ Developed an opinion about the topic
✔ Included a fact about the topic

Independent Practice Use the On Your Own activity (page 13) as review. Encourage students to use what they learned in the lesson to complete the page. Check students' work to see that they completed Part A correctly—facts: 2, 3, 4; opinions: 1, 5. Depending on levels of ability, students can dictate or write their sentences for Part B.

Name _____ Date _____

Colors

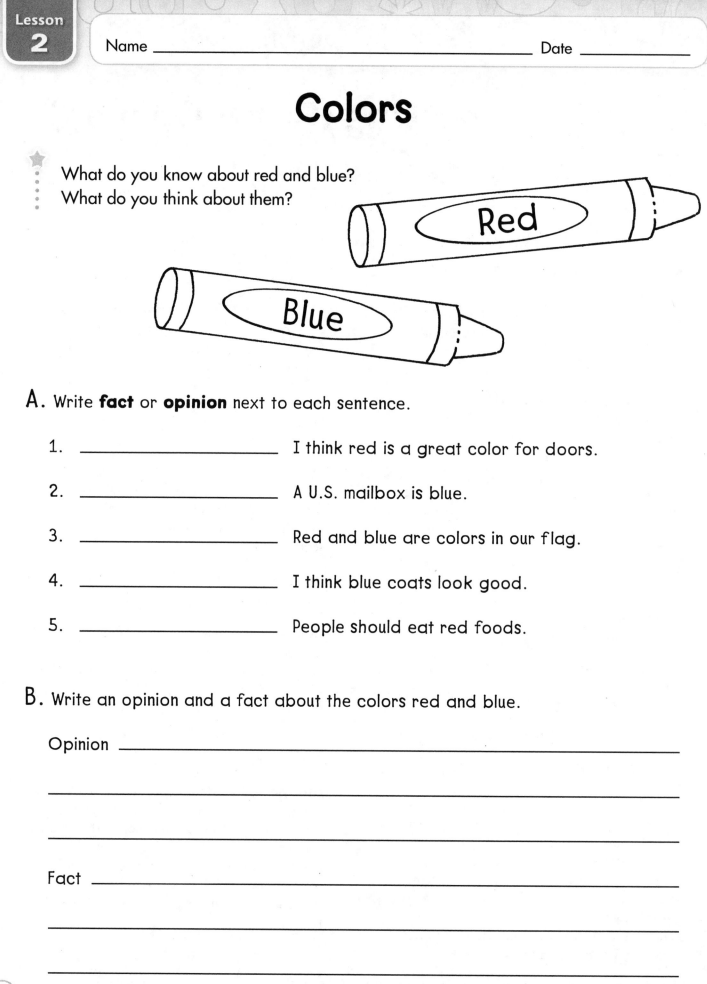

What do you know about red and blue?
What do you think about them?

A. Write **fact** or **opinion** next to each sentence.

1. _____ I think red is a great color for doors.

2. _____ A U.S. mailbox is blue.

3. _____ Red and blue are colors in our flag.

4. _____ I think blue coats look good.

5. _____ People should eat red foods.

B. Write an opinion and a fact about the colors red and blue.

Opinion _____

_____

_____

Fact _____

_____

_____

Name _____ Date _____

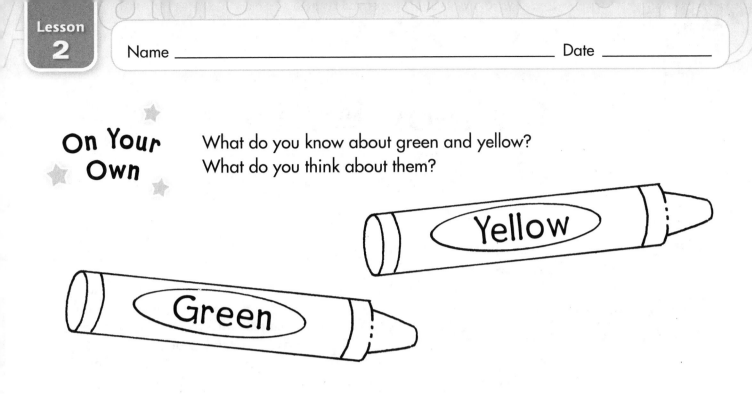

On Your Own

What do you know about green and yellow?
What do you think about them?

A. Write **fact** or **opinion** next to each sentence.

1. _____ Yellow is the best color for a room.

2. _____ Grass is green.

3. _____ A lemon is yellow.

4. _____ Green means "go" on a traffic light.

5. _____ I think green is a nice color for a T-shirt.

B. Write an opinion and a fact about the colors green and yellow.

Opinion _____

_____

_____

Fact _____

_____

_____

Opinion Writing
Fun With Faces

Objectives &
Common Core Connections

* Introduce the topic.
* Focus on the purpose of opinion writing.
* State an opinion about the topic.
* Develop a reason to support the opinion.
* Write a sentence that includes a reason for the opinion.

Introduction Provide each student with a copy of the writing frame (page 15). Read the title and first line. Also draw attention to the illustration and point out that the snowman doesn't yet have a face. Tell students to think about what kind of face they think the snowman should have. Explain that they will be writing to persuade others to agree with their opinion. Remind students that an opinion is what someone thinks or believes about something.

Model Tell students that when you write an opinion, you first introduce the topic. For example:

* You can make a face on a snowman.

Invite a volunteer to tell what kind of face he or she thinks a snowman should have. For example:

* I think a snowman should have a happy face.

Remind students that they want to persuade others to agree with their opinion. Ask: *How do you persuade someone to agree with you?* Help students understand that they should give a reason to support an opinion. For example:

* will make people smile

Guide students in developing a sentence using the reason. Review that a sentence is a group of words that tells what someone or something thinks or does. Remind students also that a sentence begins with a capital letter and usually ends with a period. For example:

* A happy face will make people smile.

Guided Practice Work with students to complete the writing frame. Tell them to draw in the face they think a snowman should have. (They can add other details, as desired.) Students should be prepared to give a reason for the kind of face they draw. Then, read aloud each direction (introduce the topic, focus on the writing purpose, state an opinion, give a reason for it, and write a practice sentence based on the reason) and help students complete the page. Depending on levels of ability, students can dictate or write their responses.

Review Invite volunteers to read their finished pages to the class. Have listeners use items 1–5 on the assessment checklist (page 62) to evaluate the effectiveness of other students' work.

Independent Practice Use the On Your Own activity (page 16) as review. Help students use what they learned in the lesson to complete the page. Explain that they can choose a face from the Idea Box or use their own face idea. Have them draw in the face before they begin writing. Depending on levels of ability, students can dictate or write their responses.

Fun With Faces

⭐ What kind of face
should a snowman have?

- Tell what the topic is.
- Tell what your writing purpose is.
- Give your opinion.
- Give a reason for it.
- Write a practice sentence.

Topic _____

_____

Writing Purpose _____

_____

Opinion _____

_____

Reason _____

_____

Practice Sentence _____

_____

On Your Own

Choose a face to draw from the Idea Box.
Or draw a different face.
Complete the page.
Get others to agree with you.

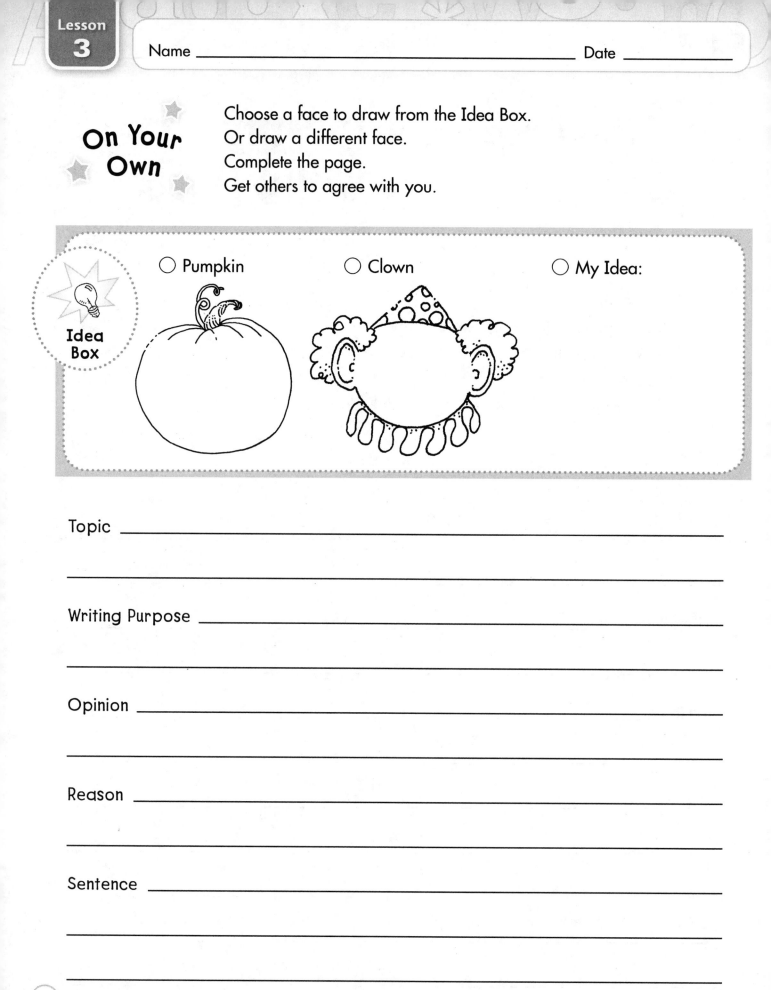

Idea Box

○ Pumpkin   ○ Clown   ○ My Idea:

Topic _____

_____

Writing Purpose _____

_____

Opinion _____

_____

Reason _____

_____

Sentence _____

_____

Opinion Writing
Stay Warm

Objectives & Common Core Connections

* Introduce the topic.
* Focus on the purpose of opinion writing.
* State an opinion about the topic.
* Develop a reason to support the opinion.
* Write a sentence that includes a reason for the opinion.

Introduction Provide each student with a copy of the writing frame (page 18). Read the title and first line. Also draw attention to the illustrations and point out that they are possible ways to keep warm. Tell students to decide what they think is the best way to stay warm. Explain that they will be writing to persuade others to agree with their opinion. Remind students that an opinion is what someone thinks or believes about something.

Model Tell students that when you write an opinion, you first introduce the topic. For example:

* People use different ways to stay warm.

Invite a volunteer to tell what he or she thinks. For example:

* Hot food is the best way to stay warm.

Remind students that they want to persuade others to agree with their opinion. Ask: *How do you persuade someone to agree with you?* Help students understand that they should give a reason to support an opinion. For example:

* warms your insides

Guide students in developing a sentence using the reason. Review that a sentence is a group of words that tells what someone or something thinks or does. Remind students also that a sentence begins with a capital letter and usually ends with a period. For example:

* Hot food makes your insides warm.

Guided Practice Work with students to complete the writing frame. Read aloud each direction (introduce the topic, focus on the writing purpose, state an opinion, give a reason for it, and write a practice sentence based on the reason) and help students complete the page. Depending on levels of ability, students can dictate or write their responses. If students wish to use one of the other ways to stay warm that are pictured, help them express an opinion and develop a reason and sentence to support it.

Review Invite volunteers to read their finished pages to the class. Have listeners use items 1–5 on the assessment checklist (page 62) to evaluate the effectiveness of other students' work.

Independent Practice Use the On Your Own activity (page 19) as review. Help students use what they learned in the lesson to complete the page. Explain that they can choose a topic from the Idea Box or use their own "Best Way" idea. Have students draw a picture of the topic reflecting their opinion before they begin writing. Depending on levels of ability, students can dictate or write their responses.

Name _____ Date _____

Stay Warm

How do you stay warm?

- Tell what the topic is.
- Tell what your writing purpose is.
- Give your opinion.
- Give a reason for it.
- Write a practice sentence.

Topic _____

_____

Writing Purpose _____

_____

Opinion _____

_____

Reason _____

_____

Practice Sentence _____

_____

_____

Writing Lessons to Meet the Common Core: Grade 1 © 2013 by Linda Ward Beech, Scholastic Teaching Resources

Name _____ Date _____

On Your Own

Choose a topic from the Idea Box.
Or think of one of your own.
Complete the page.
Get others to agree with you.

Idea Box

○ Best Way
to Stay Cool

○ Best Way
to Get to Sleep

○ My Idea:

_____

_____

_____

Topic _____

_____

Writing Purpose _____

_____

Opinion _____

_____

Reason _____

_____

Sentence _____

_____

Opinion Writing
Let's Play

Objectives & Common Core Connections

✳ Introduce the topic.

✳ Focus on the purpose of opinion writing.

✳ State an opinion about the topic.

✳ Develop a reason to support the opinion.

✳ Write a sentence that includes a reason for the opinion.

Introduction Provide each student with a copy of the writing frame (page 21). Draw attention to the illustrations and ask students where they might find this equipment (*on a playground*). Then, read the title and first line. Tell students to think about whether they like the slide or swing best. Explain that they will be writing to persuade others to agree with their opinion. Remind students that an opinion is what someone thinks or believes about something.

Model Tell students that when you write an opinion, you first introduce the topic. For example:

- You can play on different things on a playground.

Invite a volunteer to tell what he or she thinks. For example:

- I think the slide is best.

Remind students that they want to persuade others to agree with their opinion. Ask: *How do you persuade someone to agree with you?* Help students understand that they should give a reason to support an opinion. For example:

- go fast

Guide students in developing a sentence using the reason. Review that a sentence is a group of words that tells what someone or something thinks or does. Remind students also that a sentence begins with a capital letter and usually ends with a period. For example:

- You can go fast down a slide.

Guided Practice Work with students to complete the writing frame. Read aloud each direction (introduce the topic, focus on the writing purpose, state an opinion, give a reason for it, and write a sentence based on the reason) and help students complete the page. Depending on levels of ability, students can dictate or write their responses. If students choose to write about the swing, help them express an opinion and develop a reason and sentence to support it. Suggest students draw pictures showing how they enjoy the piece of equipment they write about.

Review Invite volunteers to read their finished pages to the class. Have listeners use items 1–5 on the assessment checklist (page 62) to evaluate the effectiveness of other students' work.

Independent Practice Use the On Your Own activity (page 22) as review. Help students use what they learned in the lesson to complete the page. Explain that they can choose a piece of playground equipment from the Idea Box on the page or use their own idea. Depending on levels of ability, students can dictate or write their responses. You may wish to have students copy their topic, opinion, and sentences onto another sheet of paper. Have students draw a picture of themselves on the equipment they write about.

Name _____ Date _____

Let's Play

⭐ What do you think is the best on the playground?

- Tell what the topic is.
- Tell what your writing purpose is.
- Give your opinion.
- Give a reason for it.
- Write a practice sentence.

Topic _____

_____

Writing Purpose _____

_____

Opinion _____

_____

Reason _____

_____

Practice Sentence _____

_____

_____

Name _____ Date _____

On Your Own

Choose a topic from the Idea Box.
Or think of one of your own.
Complete the page.
Get others to agree with you.

Idea Box

○ Seesaw   ○ Monkey Bars   ○ My Idea:
_____
_____

Topic _____

_____

Writing Purpose _____

_____

Opinion _____

_____

Reason _____

_____

Sentence _____

_____

_____

Opinion Writing
Seasons

Objectives & Common Core Connections

* Introduce the topic.
* Focus on the purpose of opinion writing.
* State an opinion about the topic.
* Write a sentence that includes a reason for the opinion.
* Provide a concluding statement.
* Write a simple paragraph that expresses an opinion.

Introduction Provide each student with a copy of the writing frame (page 24). Read the title and first line. Then, draw attention to the illustrations and ask students which of these seasons they like best. Explain that they will be writing to persuade others to agree with their opinion.

Model Tell students that when you write an opinion, you first introduce the topic. For example:

* Winter and summer are two of the seasons.

Invite a volunteer to tell what his or her opinion about one of the seasons is. For example:

* I think winter is a super season.

Remind students that they want to persuade others to agree with their opinion. Help students understand that they should give a reason to support an opinion. For example:

* lots of holidays

Guide students in developing a sentence using the reason. Review that a sentence is a group of words that tells what someone or something thinks or does. Remind students also that a sentence begins with a capital letter and usually ends with a period. For example:

* Winter has lots of good holidays.

Tell students that an opinion piece often has an ending sentence. For example:

* That's why I like winter best.

Guided Practice Work with students to complete the writing frame. Read aloud each direction and help students complete the page. Depending on levels of ability, students can dictate or write their responses. If students wish to write about summer, help them express an opinion and develop a reason and sentences to support it. Suggest students draw pictures of themselves enjoying the season they write about.

Review Invite volunteers to read their finished pages to the class. Have listeners use items 1–7 on the assessment checklist (page 62) to evaluate the effectiveness of other students' work.

Independent Practice Use the On Your Own activity (page 25) as review. Help students use what they learned in the lesson to complete it. Explain that they can choose a season from the Idea Box or pick a different season. Depending on levels of ability, students can dictate or write their responses. Suggest that they draw a picture of how they enjoy the season they write about on another sheet of paper.

Name _____ Date _____

Seasons

Summer

⭐ What is the best season?

- Tell what the topic and writing purpose are.
- Give your opinion.
- Write a sentence with a reason for your opinion.
- Write an ending sentence.
- Copy your work onto another sheet of paper.

Winter

Topic _____

_____

Writing Purpose _____

_____

Opinion _____

_____

Sentence With a Reason _____

_____

_____

Ending Sentence _____

_____

_____

Name _____ Date _____

On Your Own

Choose a season from the Idea Box.
Or think of another season.
Complete the page.
Get others to agree with you.
Copy your work onto another sheet of paper.

Idea Box

○ Spring   ○ Fall    ○ My Idea:

_____

_____

Topic _____

_____

Writing Purpose _____

_____

Opinion _____

_____

Sentence With a Reason _____

_____

_____

Ending Sentence _____

_____

Informative Writing (Main Idea)
Places for Fun

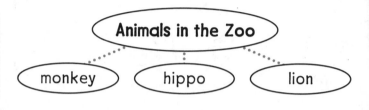

A zoo has different kinds of animals.

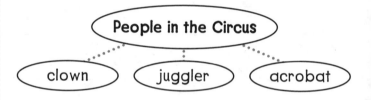

Many people perform in a circus.

Introduction Provide each student with a copy of the writing frame (page 27). Read the title and first line. Then, draw attention to the first idea web. Explain that the information in the web can be used to inform readers about what things people take to the beach.

Model You might say: Things for the Beach *would be the main idea. You can use this idea in a sentence.* Give as an example:

* You take certain things to the beach.

Point out that a writer must develop a main idea by giving more information. You might say: *The information in the smaller circles tells more about the main idea. The words* towel, umbrella, *and* pail and shovel *tell more about what specifically you might take to the beach.*

Guided Practice Help students complete the writing frame. Explain that they will write a main idea in each of the webs and then write a main idea sentence for each web. Review that a sentence is a group of words that tells what someone or something does. A sentence begins with a capital letter and usually ends with a period. Depending on levels of ability, students can write or dictate their responses. For example:

Review Invite volunteers to read their main ideas and sentences to the class. Have listeners use these criteria to assess other students' work:

✔ Identified main ideas
✔ Developed main idea sentences

Independent Practice Use the On Your Own activity (page 28) as review. Before students begin, read aloud the directions to be sure students understand them. Encourage them to use what they learned in the lesson to complete the page. Depending on levels of ability, students can write or dictate their responses.

Name _____ Date _____

Places for Fun

Where can you have fun?

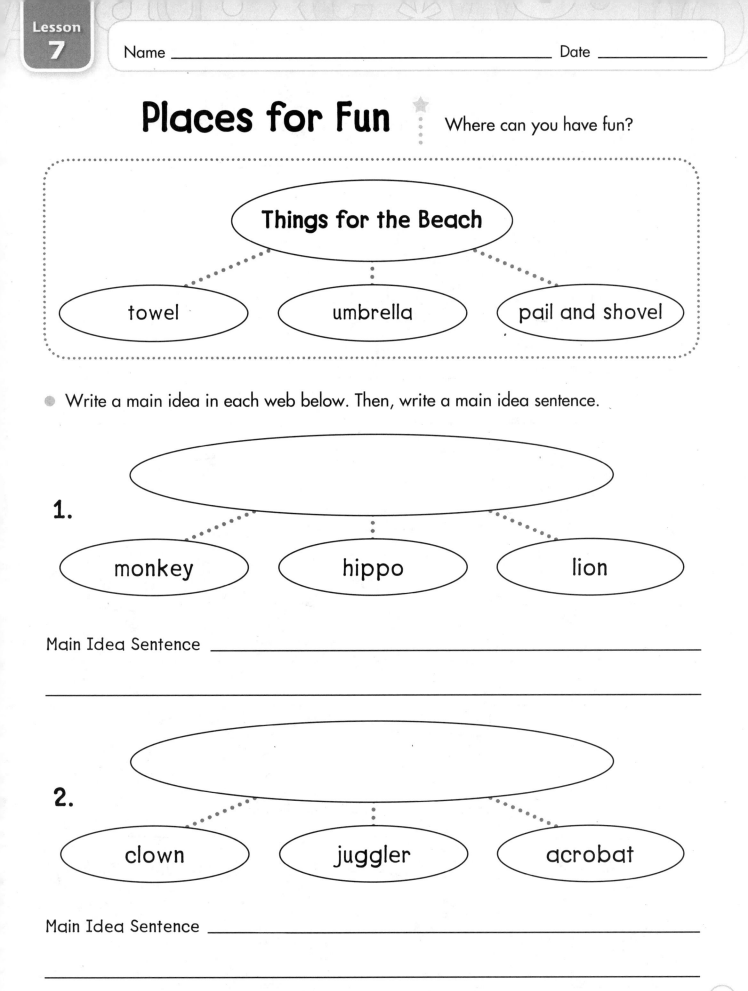

Things for the Beach

towel

umbrella

pail and shovel

● Write a main idea in each web below. Then, write a main idea sentence.

1.

monkey

hippo

lion

Main Idea Sentence _____

_____

2.

clown

juggler

acrobat

Main Idea Sentence _____

_____

Name _____ Date _____

On Your Own

Write a main idea in each web below. Then, write a main idea sentence.

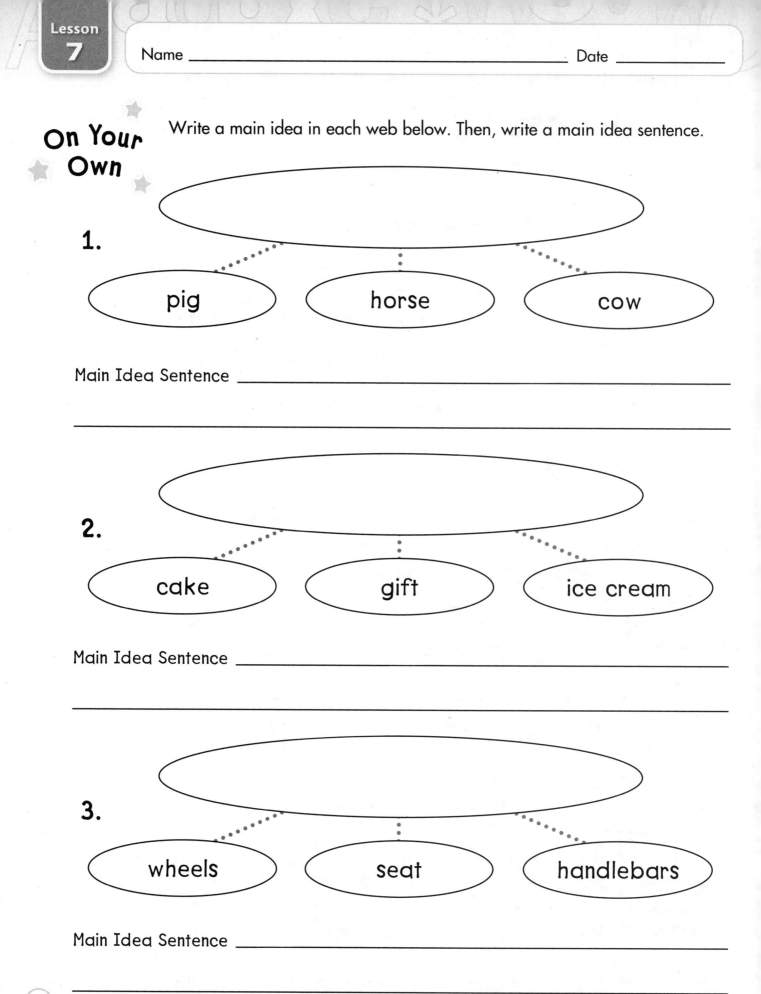

1.

pig   horse   cow

Main Idea Sentence _____

_____

2.

cake   gift   ice cream

Main Idea Sentence _____

_____

3.

wheels   seat   handlebars

Main Idea Sentence _____

_____

Informative Writing (Main Idea)
Things to Wear

Objectives & Common Core Connections

* Identify main ideas.
* Develop main idea sentences about topics.

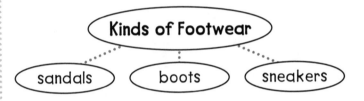

People wear many kinds of hats.

There are many kinds of footwear to wear on your feet.

Introduction Provide each student with a copy of the writing frame (page 30). Read the title and first line. Then, draw attention to the first idea web. Explain that the information in the web can be used in a paragraph to inform readers about kinds of jewelry.

Model You might say: Kinds of Jewelry *would be the main idea. You can use this idea in a sentence.* Give as an example:

* People wear different kinds of jewelry.

Point out that a writer must develop a main idea by giving more information. You might say: *The information in the smaller circles tells more about the main idea. The words* ring, pin, *and* watch *tell more about kinds of jewelry.*

Guided Practice Help students complete the writing frame. Explain that they will write a main idea in each of the webs and then write a main idea sentence for each web. Review that a sentence is a group of words that tells what someone or something does. A sentence begins with a capital letter and usually ends with a period. Depending on levels of ability, students can write or dictate their responses. For example:

Review Invite volunteers to read their main ideas and sentences to the class. Have listeners use these criteria to assess other students' work:

✔ Identified main ideas
✔ Developed main idea sentences

Independent Practice Use the On Your Own activity (page 31) as review. Before students begin, read aloud the directions to be sure students understand them. Encourage them to use what they learned in the lesson to complete the page. Depending on levels of ability, students can write or dictate their responses.

Name _____ Date _____

Things to Wear

What kinds of things do people wear?

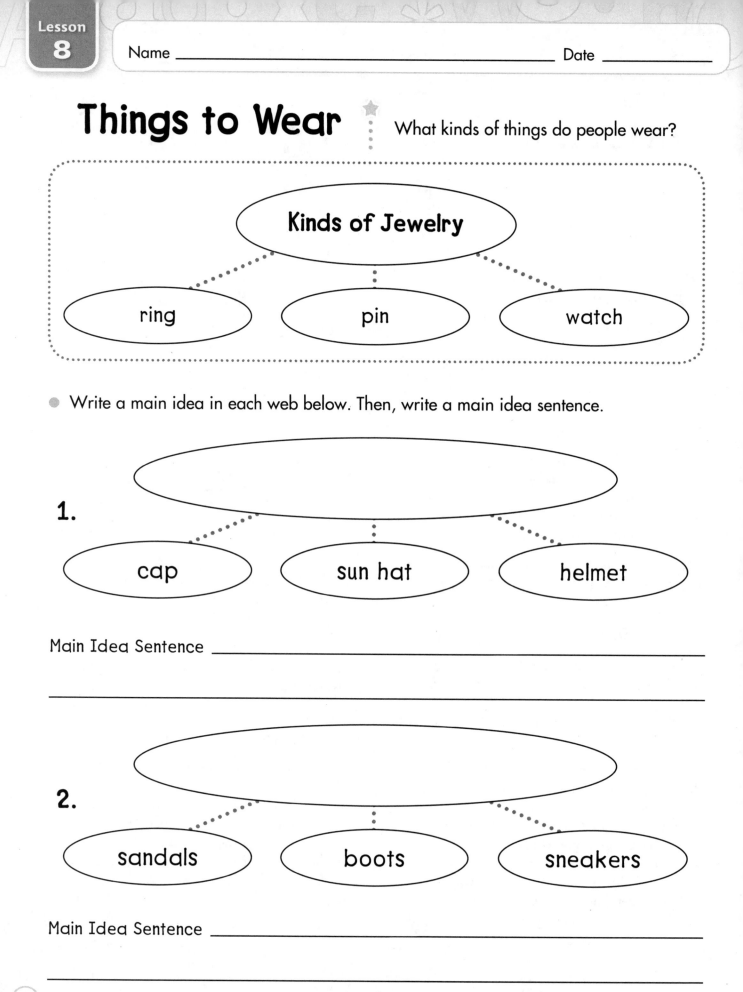

Kinds of Jewelry

ring   pin   watch

● Write a main idea in each web below. Then, write a main idea sentence.

1.

cap   sun hat   helmet

Main Idea Sentence _____

_____

2.

sandals   boots   sneakers

Main Idea Sentence _____

_____

Name _____ Date _____

On Your Own

Write a main idea in each web below. Then, write a main idea sentence.

1.

(lettuce) (tomatoes) (carrots)

Main Idea Sentence _____

_____

2.

(crib) (rattle) (bottle)

Main Idea Sentence _____

_____

3.

(whale) (shark) (seal)

Main Idea Sentence _____

_____

Informative Writing
Apples

Objectives & Common Core Connections

✳ Introduce a topic with a main idea sentence.

✳ Focus on the purpose of informative writing.

✳ Use facts to develop the topic.

✳ Write sentences using the facts.

Introduction Provide each student with a copy of the writing frame (page 33). Read the title and first line. Also draw attention to the illustrations. Tell students they will write sentences to tell what an apple is. Discuss the purpose of informative writing.

Model You might say: *The picture shows an apple. That will be the topic we will write about. We can introduce the topic by writing a main idea sentence such as:*

• An apple is a fruit.

Explain that the next step is to tell more about the topic. Remind students that their purpose is to inform or tell more about the topic. Suggest that they use the illustrations and their own knowledge for more information. For example:

• grows on a tree

• can hold in your hand to eat

Encourage students to contribute other information about apples, then coach them in using the information to develop complete sentences. Review that a sentence is a group of words that tells what someone or something does. A sentence begins with a capital letter and usually ends with a period. For example:

• An apple grows on a tree.

• You can hold an apple in your hand to eat it.

Guided Practice Help students complete the writing frame. Read aloud each direction and guide students in completing it. Encourage them to use their own words and sentences when they write their practice sentences. Depending on levels of ability, students can write or dictate their responses.

Review Invite volunteers to share their pages with the class. Have listeners use items 1–3 on the assessment checklist (page 63) to evaluate the effectiveness of other students' work.

Independent Practice Use the On Your Own activity (page 34) as review. Encourage students to use what they learned in the lesson to complete the page. Explain that they can choose a fruit from the Idea Box or choose another fruit. Depending on levels of ability, students can write or dictate their responses.

Writing Lessons to Meet the Common Core: Grade 1 © 2013 by Linda Ward Beech, Scholastic Teaching Resources

Name _____ Date _____

Apples

⭐ What is an apple?

- Tell what the topic is.
- Tell what your writing purpose is.
- Write a main idea sentence.
- List facts about the topic.
- Write practice sentences.

Topic _____

Writing Purpose _____

_____

Main Idea Sentence _____

_____

Facts _____

_____

_____

_____

Practice Sentences _____

_____

_____

_____

_____

Name _____ Date _____

On Your Own

Choose a fruit from the Idea Box.
Or think of another fruit.
Complete the page to tell what the fruit is like.

Idea Box

○ Banana   ○ Grapes    ○ My Idea:

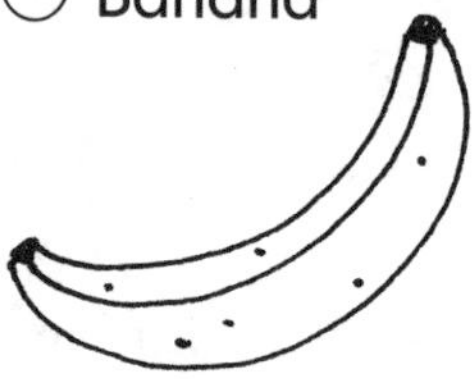

_____

Topic _____

Writing Purpose _____

_____

Main Idea Sentence _____

_____

Facts _____

_____

_____

_____

Sentences _____

_____

_____

_____

_____

Explanatory Writing
Make a Snack

Objectives & Common Core Connections

* Introduce a topic with a main idea sentence.
* Focus on the purpose of explanatory writing.
* List materials and steps.
* Write a simple explanatory paragraph.

Introduction Provide each student with a copy of the writing frame (page 36). Read the title and first line. Also have students study the illustration. Tell them that they will write an explanation of how to make a snack called Ants on a Log using celery, cream cheese, and raisins. Discuss the purpose of explanatory writing—to tell a reader how to make or do something.

Model Help students begin their explanation by writing a main idea sentence. For example:

* You can make a snack called Ants on a Log.

Tell students that when explaining how to do something, they should list the materials needed and tell what steps to take. For example:

* get a celery stick, cream cheese, raisins, knife, napkin
* put cream cheese on celery
* add raisins

Coach students in developing complete sentences to write an explanatory paragraph. For example:

* Get a celery stick, cream cheese, and raisins.
* Get a knife and a napkin.
* Put the celery on a napkin.
* Spread the cream cheese on the celery.
* Put raisins on top.

Guided Practice Help students complete the writing frame. Read aloud each direction and guide students in completing it. Encourage them to use their own words and sentences. Depending on levels of ability, students can write or dictate their work. (If you make this snack with your class, use plastic knives.)

Review Invite volunteers to read their finished sentences to the class. Have listeners use items 1, 2, 4, and 6 on the assessment checklist (page 63) to evaluate the effectiveness of other students' work.

Independent Practice Use the On Your Own activity (page 37) as review. Encourage students to use what they learned in the lesson to complete the page. Explain that they can choose the snack from the Idea Box or use their own idea. Students might want to draw their idea on a separate sheet of paper first. Depending on levels of ability, they can write, dictate, or draw their explanations. (To make the Snowman Snack shown in the Idea Box, you need: large and small round crackers, cottage cheese, spoons, and shelled sunflower seeds.)

Writing Lessons to Meet the Common Core: Grade 1 © 2013 by Linda Ward Beech, Scholastic Teaching Resources

Name _____ Date _____

Make a Snack

How can you make a snack?

- Tell what your topic is.
- Tell what your writing purpose is.
- Write a main idea sentence
- List what you need.
- Tell how to make a snack.

Topic _____

Writing Purpose _____

_____

Main Idea Sentence _____

_____

What You Need _____

_____

_____

What to Do _____

_____

_____

_____

_____

Name _____ Date _____

On Your Own

Complete the page to tell how to make a Snowman Snack.
Or think of your own snack idea.

Idea Box

○ Snowman Snack   ○ My Idea:

_____

_____

_____

Topic _____

Writing Purpose _____

_____

Main Idea Sentence _____

_____

What You Need _____

_____

_____

What to Do _____

_____

_____

Explanatory Writing
Draw a Turkey

Objectives & Common Core Connections

* Introduce a topic with a main idea sentence.
* Focus on the purpose of explanatory writing.
* List materials and steps.
* Write a simple explanatory paragraph.

Introduction Provide each student with a copy of the writing frame (page 39). Read the title and first line. Also have students study the illustrations. Tell them that they will write an explanation of how to draw a turkey.

Model Help students begin their explanation by writing a main idea sentence. For example:

* Here is how to draw a turkey.

Tell students that when explaining how to do something, they should list the materials needed and tell what to do. For example:

* get paper and pencil
* trace hand on the paper
* draw eyes and beak on the thumb

Point out that the steps must be given in a logical order so someone can follow them. Coach students in developing complete and more informative sentences to write an explanatory text. For example:

* Collect paper and a pencil.
* Trace your hand on the paper.
* Draw eyes and a beak on the thumb.

Guided Practice Help students complete the writing frame. Read aloud each direction and guide students in following it. Encourage them to use their own words and sentence structure. Depending on levels of ability, students can write or dictate their work. You may wish to have them copy their main idea sentences, materials, and steps onto another sheet of paper. Some students may wish to include step-by-step pictures to show how to draw a turkey and add other details as desired.

Review Invite volunteers to read their finished sentences to the class. Have listeners use items 1, 2, 4, and 6 on the assessment checklist (page 63) to evaluate the effectiveness of other students' work.

Independent Practice Use the On Your Own activity (page 40) as review. Encourage students to use what they learned in the lesson to complete it. Explain that they can choose the sheep from the Idea Box or use their own idea. Students might want to draw their idea on a separate sheet of paper first. Depending on levels of ability, they can write, dictate, or draw their responses.

Draw a Turkey

⭐ How can you draw a turkey?

- Tell what the topic is.
- Tell what your writing purpose is.
- Write a main idea sentence.
- List what you need.
- Tell how to draw a turkey.

Topic _____

Writing Purpose _____

_____

Main Idea Sentence _____

_____

What You Need _____

_____

What to Do _____

_____

_____

_____

_____

Name _____ Date _____

On Your Own

Complete the page to tell how to draw a sheep.
Or think of your own idea for drawing something.

Idea Box

○ Sheep   ○ My Idea:

_____

_____

_____

_____

Topic _____

Writing Purpose _____

_____

Main Idea Sentence _____

_____

What You Need _____

_____

What to Do _____

_____

_____

Informative Writing
Sort It Out

Objectives & Common Core Connections

* Introduce a topic with a main idea sentence.
* Focus on the purpose of informative writing.
* Write sentences using facts to develop the topic.
* Provide a concluding statement.
* Write an informative paragraph.

Introduction Provide each student with a copy of the writing frame (page 42). Read the title and first line. Also have students study the illustration. Tell them they will write an informative paragraph about recycling. Discuss the purpose of informative writing.

Model You might say: *The picture shows a recycling center in a classroom. That is the topic we will write about. We can introduce the topic by writing a main idea sentence such as:*

* You can recycle things in your classroom.

Explain that the next step is to tell more about the topic. Remind students that their purpose is to inform their readers. Suggest that they use the illustration and their own knowledge and experience for more information. For example:

* recycle paper
* recycle glass
* recycle metal

Coach students in using the information to develop complete sentences. For example:

* Put paper in one bin.
* Put glass in a different bin.
* Put metal in another bin.

Tell students that an informative text often has an ending sentence that tells more about the topic. For example:

* You recycle things so they can be used again.

Guided Practice Help students complete the writing frame. Read aloud each direction and guide students in following it. Encourage them to use their own words and sentences. Depending on levels of ability, students can write or dictate their work.

Review Invite volunteers to read their finished sentences to the class. Have listeners use items 1–3, 5, and 6 on the assessment checklist (page 63) to evaluate the effectiveness of other students' work.

Independent Practice Use the On Your Own activity (page 43) as review. Encourage students to use what they learned in the lesson to complete it. Explain that they can choose the sorting activity from the Idea Box or use their own idea. Depending on levels of ability, students can write or dictate their sentences.

Name _____ Date _____

Sort It Out

How can you recycle?

- Tell what the topic is.
- Tell what your writing purpose is.
- Write a main idea sentence and sentences with facts.
- Write an ending sentence.
- Copy your work onto another sheet of paper.

Topic _____

Writing Purpose _____

_____

Main Idea Sentence _____

_____

Sentences With Facts _____

_____

_____

_____

_____

Ending Sentence _____

_____

On Your Own

Complete the page to tell how to sort the books on the shelves.
Or think of your own sorting idea.
Copy your work onto another sheet of paper.

Idea Box

○ Bookshelf   ○ My Idea:

HUMAN BODY

ANIMALS

OUTER SPACE

Our Moon

All About Ants

The Five Senses

_____

_____

_____

Topic _____

Writing Purpose _____

_____

Main Idea Sentence _____

_____

Sentences With Facts _____

_____

_____

_____

_____

Ending Sentence _____

Narrative Writing (Sequence)
Story Order

Introduction Provide each student with a copy of the writing frame (page 45). Read the title and first line. Also draw attention to the illustrations. Point out that the pictures show a series of events in the order, or sequence, in which they happened. Tell students that when you write a story, you use sequence to help the reader understand what is happening. Explain that if you tell things out of order, they don't make sense.

Model You might say: *You can make up a story based on what you see in the pictures. Authors write stories to entertain readers.* Have students follow along as you read aloud the sample sentences under the pictures at the top of the page. Explain that if the pictures and sentences were out of order, the story wouldn't make much sense.

Guided Practice Help students complete the writing frame. Guide them in determining the best order for the three pictures at the bottom of the page and have them number the pictures accordingly (3, 2, 1). Then, discuss what is happening in each picture in the correct order:

• got toothbrush (Picture C)

• put on toothpaste (Picture B)

• brushed teeth (Picture A)

Next, help students develop a sentence for each picture. Point out that you are going to give the alligator in the pictures a name—Allie. For example:

1. Allie got his toothbrush.

2. He put toothpaste on it.

3. Allie brushed his teeth.

Review Invite volunteers to read their sentences to the class. Have listeners use these criteria to assess other students' work:

✔ Identified sequence of events for a narrative

✔ Wrote sentences and read them in sequence

Independent Practice Use the On Your Own activity (page 46) as review. Encourage students to use what they learned in the lesson to complete the page. Point out that they should first number the pictures in order (3, 1, 2), and then develop a sentence for each. Invite students to give the boy and girl in the pictures names. Depending on levels of ability, they can write or dictate their sentences. Note: To make it easier for students to read their sentences in sequence, you might have them cut apart the pictures and accompanying sentences and then glue them, in order, to another sheet of paper.

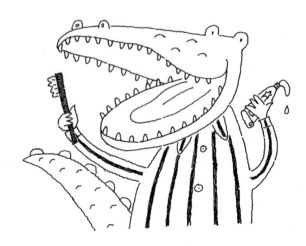

Name _____ Date _____

Story Order

The pictures below tell a story in order.

Snail wanted to cross the pond.	**1**

Snail made a raft.	**2**

Snail sailed across the pond.	**3**

● Number the pictures in order to tell a story. Then, write a sentence for each picture.

A

B

Here is my toothbrush.

C

_____   _____   _____

_____   _____   _____

_____   _____   _____

On Your Own

Number the pictures in order to tell a story.
Then, write a sentence for each picture.

Writing Lessons to Meet the Common Core: Grade 1 © 2013 by Linda Ward Beech, Scholastic Teaching Resources

Narrative Writing (Sequence)
Time to Eat

Introduction Provide each student with a copy of the writing frame (page 48). Read the title and first line. Also draw attention to the illustrations. Point out that the pictures show a series of events in the order, or sequence, in which they happened. Tell students that when you write a story, you use sequence to help the reader understand what is happening. Explain that if you tell things out of order, they don't make sense.

Model You might say: *You can make up a story based on what you see in the pictures. Authors write stories to entertain readers.* Have students follow along as you read aloud the sample sentences under the pictures at the top of the page. Discuss how the story wouldn't make sense if the pictures and sentences were out of order.

Guided Practice Help students complete the writing frame. Guide them in determining the best order for the three pictures along the side of the page and have them number the pictures accordingly (1, 3, 2). Discuss what is happening in each picture in the correct order:

- got dog food (Picture A)
- filled dish (Picture C)
- put dish on floor for dog (Picture B)

Next, help students develop a sentence for each picture. Point out that you are going to give a name to the girl (Baya) and to the dog (Lucky) in the pictures. For example:

1. Baya got out the dog food.
2. She filled Lucky's dish.
3. Baya put the dish on the floor for Lucky.

Review Invite volunteers to read their sentences to the class. Have listeners use these criteria to assess other students' work:

✔ Identified sequence of events for a narrative
✔ Wrote sentences and read them in sequence

Independent Practice Use the On Your Own activity (page 49) as review. Encourage students to use what they learned in the lesson to complete the page. Point out that they should first number the pictures in order (2, 3, 1), and then develop a sentence for each. Tell students they can also name the girl and the woman in the pictures, if they like. Depending on levels of ability, students can write or dictate their sentences. Note: To make it easier for students to read their sentences in sequence, you might have them cut apart the pictures and accompanying sentences and then glue them, in order, to another sheet of paper.

Time to Eat

The pictures below tell a story in order.

Dad took the pot off the stove. **1**	He filled Taylor's bowl with soup. **2**	He put the bowl on the table. **3**

● Number the pictures in order to tell a story.
● Then, write a sentence for each picture.

A

_____
_____
_____

B

_____
_____
_____

C

_____
_____
_____

Name _____ Date _____

On Your Own

Number the pictures in order to tell a story.
Then, write a sentence for each picture.

Narrative Writing
Surprise!

Objectives & Common Core Connections

* Focus on the purpose of narrative writing.
* Write sentences in sequence to recount events.
* Write a narrative.

Introduction Provide each student with a copy of the writing frame (page 51). Read the title and first line. Also draw attention to the illustrations. Tell students that they will write a narrative about what is happening in the pictures. Review that a narrative is a story or an account of something that is written to entertain the reader. Tell students that when you write a narrative, you use sequence to help the reader understand what is happening.

Model You might say: *You can make up sentences for a story or narrative based on these pictures.* Begin by inviting students to describe what each picture shows. For example:

* Bear sees gift.
* Bear opens gift.
* Bear goes to sleep with teddy bear.

Have students follow the pictures as you suggest sample sentences for each one. For example:

* In winter, Bear saw a gift under a tree.
* Bear opened the gift and took out a teddy bear!
* Bear went to sleep in a cave with the teddy bear.

Guided Practice Help students complete the writing frame. Read aloud each direction and guide students in following it. Coach them in stating their writing purpose. Depending on levels of ability, students can write or dictate the sentences. Encourage them to use their own words and sentences.

Review Invite volunteers to read their sentences to the class. Have listeners use items 1, 2, and 6 on the assessment checklist (page 64) to evaluate the effectiveness of other students' work.

Independent Practice Use the On Your Own activity (page 52) as review. Encourage students to use what they learned in the lesson to complete the page. Tell them they can choose a topic about a surprise from the Idea Box or think of one of their own. Suggest that they draw three pictures on separate sheets of paper to illustrate their narrative first and then write a sentence for each picture. Depending on levels of ability, students can write or dictate their sentences. You might also invite them to title their stories.

Name _____ Date _____

Surprise! Use the pictures to tell a story.

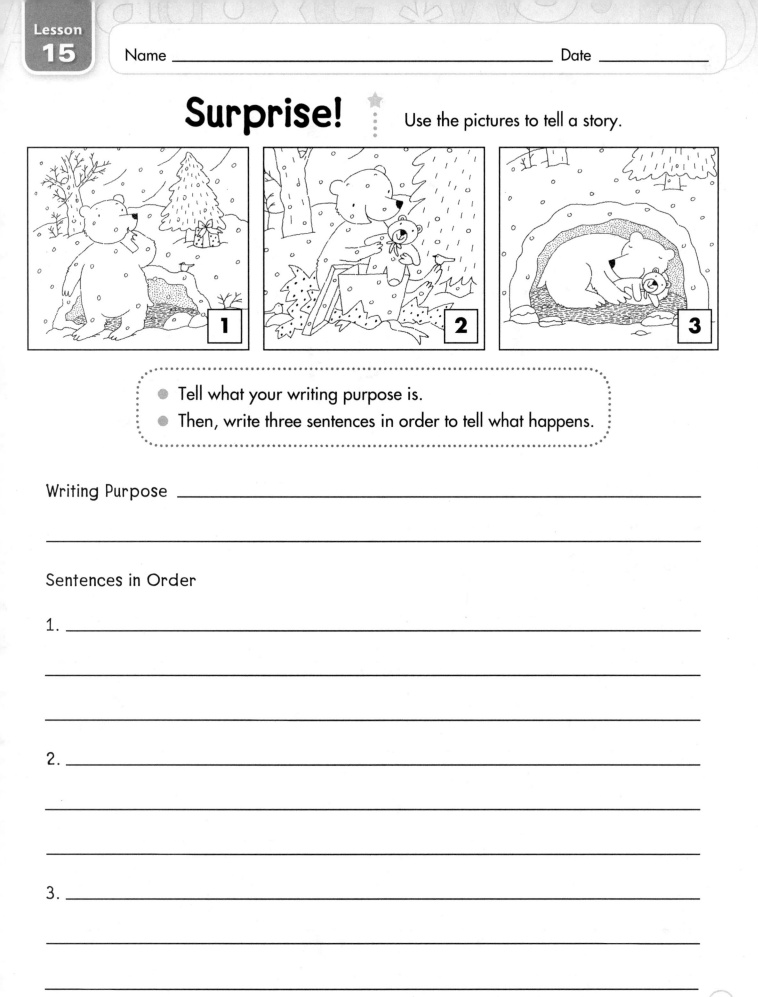

- Tell what your writing purpose is.
- Then, write three sentences in order to tell what happens.

Writing Purpose _____

_____

Sentences in Order

1. _____

_____

_____

2. _____

_____

_____

3. _____

_____

Name _____ Date _____

On Your Own

Choose a story idea from the Idea Box.
Or think of your own idea.
Complete the page to tell the story.

Idea Box

○ A Visit From
the Tooth Fairy

○ A Cat's Lost
Toy Mouse

○ My Idea:

_____

_____

Writing Purpose _____

_____

Sentences in Order

1. _____

_____

_____

2. _____

_____

_____

3. _____

_____

_____

Narrative Writing
YaYa's Day

Objectives & Common Core Connections

* Focus on the purpose of narrative writing.
* Write sentences in sequence to recount events.
* Write sentences with details.
* Write a narrative.

Introduction Provide each student with a copy of the writing frame (page 54). Read the title and first line. Also draw attention to the illustrations. Tell students that they will write a narrative about what is happening in the pictures. Review that a narrative is a story or an account of something that is written to entertain the reader. Tell students that when you write a narrative, you use sequence to help the reader understand what is happening.

Model You might say: *You can make up sentences for a story or narrative based on these pictures.* Begin by inviting students to describe what each picture shows. For example:

* panda eating bamboo
* two pandas playing
* pandas sleeping

Have students follow the pictures as you suggest sample sentences for each one. Explain that you're going to begin by giving names to the pandas in the pictures—YaYa and YoYo. Tell students that you will also include details to give more information to the reader. Write each sentence and then go back and add the details (underlined below). For example:

* YaYa ate some bamboo <u>for a snack</u>.
* He played with YoYo <u>for a long time</u>.
* The pandas took a nap <u>in a tree</u>.

Guided Practice Help students complete the writing frame. Read aloud each direction and guide students in following it. Coach them in stating their writing purpose. Depending on levels of ability, students can write or dictate their sentences. Encourage them to use their own words and sentences and to underline the details they add.

Review Invite volunteers to read their sentences to the class. Have listeners use items 1–3 and 6 on the assessment checklist (page 64) to evaluate the effectiveness of other students' work.

Independent Practice Use the On Your Own activity (page 55) as review. Encourage students to use what they learned in the lesson to complete the page. Tell them they can choose an animal from the Idea Box or think of one of their own. Suggest to students that they draw three pictures on separate sheets of paper to illustrate their narrative first and then write a sentence for each picture. Remind them to underline the details they add. Depending on levels of ability, students can write or dictate their sentences. You might also invite them to title their stories.

YaYa's Day

Use the pictures to tell a story.

- Tell what your writing purpose is.
- Write three sentences in order to tell what happens.
- Use details.

Writing Purpose _____

_____

Sentences in Order

1. _____

_____

_____

2. _____

_____

_____

3. _____

_____

On Your Own

Choose an animal from the Idea Box.
Or think of another animal.
Complete the page to tell a story about the animal's day.
Use details.

Idea Box

○ Tiger   ○ Camel   ○ My Idea:

_____

_____

Writing Purpose _____

_____

Sentences in Order

1. _____

_____

_____

2. _____

_____

_____

3. _____

_____

_____

Narrative Writing
Molly's Book

Objectives & Common Core Connections

* Focus on the purpose of narrative writing.
* Write sentences in sequence to recount events.
* Write sentences with details.
* Use temporal words to signal event order.
* Write a narrative.

Introduction Provide each student with a copy of the writing frame (page 57). Read the title and first line. Also draw attention to the illustrations. Tell students that they will write a narrative about what is happening in the pictures. Review that a narrative is a story or an account of something that is written to entertain the reader. A narrative can be about something that really happened, or it can be make-believe (like the story on this page). Tell students that when you write a narrative, you use sequence to help the reader understand what is happening. Using time words helps show the sequence of events.

Model You might say: *You can make up sentences for a story or narrative based on these pictures.* Begin by inviting students to describe what each picture shows. For example:

* doll jumps off bed
* doll gets book
* doll reads book

Have students follow the pictures as you suggest sample sentences for each one. Explain that you're going to begin by giving a name to the doll in the pictures—Molly. Tell students that you will also include details to give more information to the reader. Write each

sentence and then go back and add the details (underlined below). Also introduce the use of time words, such as *first*, *next*, and *then*. Explain that these words help a reader understand sequence in a text. Circle the time words in each sentence. For example:

* (First,) Molly jumped off the bed.
* (Next,) she got a book from the shelf.
* (Then,) she sat on a chair to read.

Guided Practice Help students complete the writing frame. Begin by asking them to write a time word under each picture to indicate its sequence in the story. Then, read aloud each direction and guide students in following it. Coach them in stating their writing purpose. Depending on levels of ability, students can write or dictate their sentences. Encourage them to use their own words and sentences and to underline the details and circle the time words they add.

Review Invite volunteers to read their sentences to the class. Have listeners use items 1–4 and 6 on the assessment checklist (page 64) to evaluate the effectiveness of other students' work.

Independent Practice Use the On Your Own activity (page 58) as review. Encourage students to use what they learned in the lesson to complete the page. Tell them they can choose a toy from the Idea Box or think of one of their own. Suggest that students draw three pictures on separate sheets of paper to illustrate their narrative first and then write a sentence for each picture. Remind them to underline the details and circle the time words. Depending on levels of ability, students can write or dictate their sentences. You might also invite them to title their stories.

Name _____ Date _____

Molly's Book

Use the pictures to tell a story.

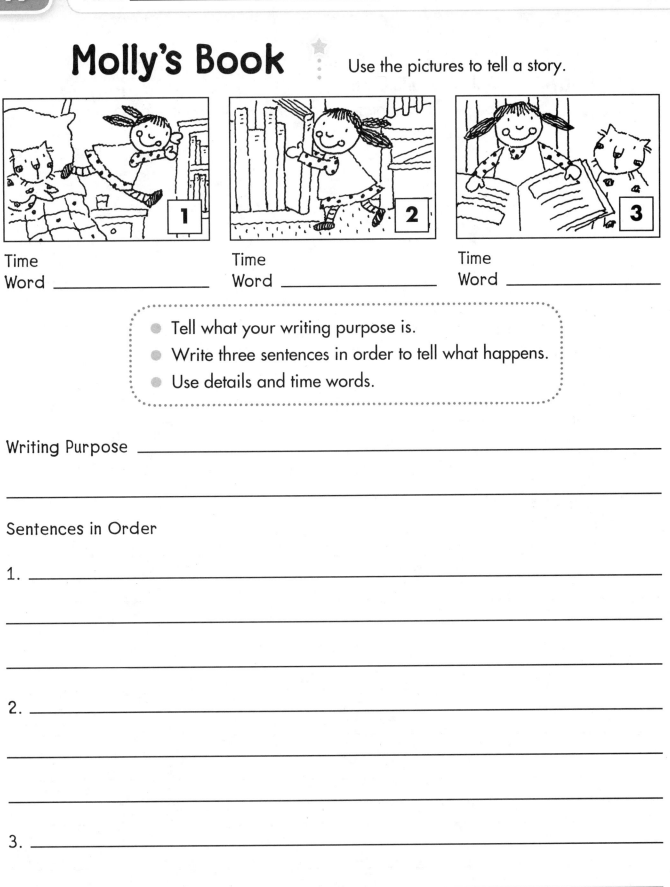

Time
Word _____

Time
Word _____

Time
Word _____

- Tell what your writing purpose is.
- Write three sentences in order to tell what happens.
- Use details and time words.

Writing Purpose _____

_____

Sentences in Order

1. _____

_____

_____

2. _____

_____

_____

3. _____

_____

Name _____ Date _____

On Your Own

Choose a toy from the Idea Box.
Or think of another toy.
Complete the page to tell a story about something the toy does.
Use details and time words.

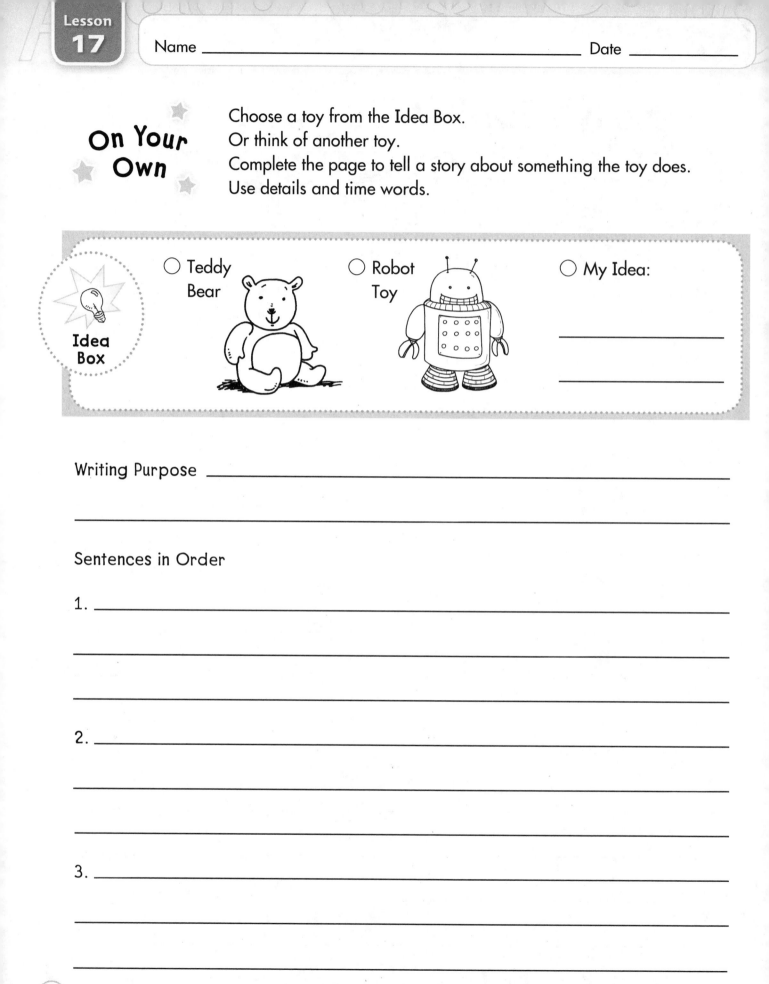

Idea Box

○ Teddy Bear   ○ Robot Toy   ○ My Idea:

_____

_____

Writing Purpose _____

_____

Sentences in Order

1. _____

_____

_____

2. _____

_____

_____

3. _____

_____

_____

Narrative Writing
Pepe's Pet

Objectives & Common Core Connections

* Focus on the purpose of narrative writing.
* Write sentences in sequence to recount events.
* Write sentences with details.
* Use temporal words to signal event order.
* Provide a conclusion.
* Write a narrative.

Introduction Provide each student with a copy of the writing frame (page 60). Read the title and first line. Also draw attention to the illustrations. Tell students that they will write a narrative about what is happening in the pictures. Review that a narrative is a story or an account of something that is written to entertain the reader. A narrative can be about something that really happened, or it can be make-believe (like the story on this page). Tell students that when you write a narrative, you use sequence to help the reader understand what is happening. Using time words helps show the sequence of events.

Model You might say: *You can make up sentences for a story or narrative based on these pictures.* Begin by inviting students to describe what each picture shows. For example:

* boy opens box with baby dinosaur
* boy puts dinosaur in wagon
* dinosaur rides in back of pickup truck
* boy rides on dinosaur's back

Have students follow the pictures as you suggest sample sentences for each one. Explain that you're going to begin by giving a name to the boy in the pictures—Pepe. Tell students that you

will also include details to give more information to the reader. Write each sentence and then go back and add the details (underlined below). Review the use of time words, such as *then* and *now*, and circle them. For example:

* Pepe got a baby dinosaur <u>for his birthday</u>.
* He liked to take it for rides <u>in a wagon</u>.
* (Then,) the dinosaur <u>grew too big</u>.

Point out that a story has an ending or conclusion. Give as an example:

* (Now,) the dinosaur takes Pepe for rides!

Guided Practice Help students complete the writing frame. Read aloud each direction and guide them in following it. Coach students in stating their writing purpose. Depending on levels of ability, they can write or dictate their sentences. Encourage students to use their own words and sentences and to underline the details and circle the time words they add.

Review Invite volunteers to read their sentences to the class. Have listeners use items 1–6 on the assessment checklist (page 64) to evaluate the effectiveness of other students' work.

Independent Practice Use the On Your Own activity (page 61) as review. Encourage students to use what they learned in the lesson to complete the page. Tell them they can choose a make-believe pet from the Idea Box or think of one of their own. Suggest that students draw four pictures on separate sheets of paper to illustrate their narrative first and then write a sentence for each picture. Remind them to underline the details and circle the time words. Depending on levels of ability, students can write or dictate their sentences. You might also invite them to title their stories.

Name _____ Date _____

Pepe's Pet

Use the pictures to tell a story.

- Tell what your writing purpose is.
- Write three sentences in order to tell what happens.
- Use details and time words.
- Write an ending sentence.

Writing Purpose _____

Sentences in Order

1. _____

_____

_____

2. _____

_____

_____

3. _____

_____

_____

Ending Sentence _____

_____

Writing Lessons to Meet the Common Core: Grade 1 © 2013 by Linda Ward Beech, Scholastic Teaching Resources

Name _____ Date _____

On Your Own

Choose a make-believe pet from the Idea Box.
Or think of your own idea.
Complete the page to tell a story about the pet.
Use details and time words.

Idea Box

○ Dragon   ○ Unicorn    ○ My Idea:

_____

_____

Writing Purpose _____

Sentences in Order

1. _____

_____

_____

2. _____

_____

_____

3. _____

_____

_____

Ending Sentence _____

_____

Student Assessment Checklist
Opinion Writing

1. Told what the topic is. .... ☐

2. Understood the writing purpose. .... ☐

3. Wrote an opinion sentence. .... ☐

4. Gave a reason for the opinion. .... ☐

5. Wrote sentences with reasons. .... ☐

6. Added an ending sentence. .... ☐

7. Wrote a paragraph that gives an opinion. ...... ☐

More Things to Check

● Capital Letters ☐

● Periods ☐

● Spelling ☐

Student Assessment Checklist
Informative/Explanatory Writing

1. Wrote a main idea sentence to tell what the topic is. .... ☐

2. Understood the writing purpose. .... ☐

3. Wrote sentences with facts. .... ☐

4. Listed the materials and steps. .... ☐

5. Wrote an ending sentence. .... ☐

6. Wrote an informative/explanatory paragraph. .... ☐

More Things to Check

● Capital Letters ☐

● Periods ☐

● Spelling ☐

Name _____ Date _____

Student Assessment Checklist
Narrative Writing

1. Understood the writing purpose. .... ☐

2. Wrote two or more sentences in order to tell what happens. .... ☐

3. Wrote sentences with details. .... ☐

4. Used time words. .... ☐

5. Wrote an ending sentence. .... ☐

6. Wrote a narrative (story). .... ☐

More Things to Check

• Capital Letters ☐

• Periods ☐

• Spelling ☐

Writing Lessons to Meet the Common Core: Grade 1 © 2013 by Linda Ward Beech, Scholastic Teaching Resources